RANDY'S CORNER

DAY BY DAY WITH...

SHAUN WHITE

BY
TAMMY GAGNE

Mitchell Lane

PUBLISHERS

P.O. Box 196
Hockessin, Delaware 19707
Visit us on the web: www.mitchelllane.com
Comments? email us:
mitchelllane@mitchelllane.com

Mitchell Lane
PUBLISHERS

Printing   1   2   3   4   5   6   7   8   9

RANDY'S CORNER

DAY BY DAY WITH. . .

Beyoncé	Miley Cyrus
Dwayne "The Rock" Johnson	Selena Gomez
Eli Manning	Shaun White
Justin Bieber	Taylor Swift
LeBron James	Willow Smith

Library of Congress Cataloging-in-Publication Data
Gagne, Tammy.
 Day by day with Shaun White / by Tammy Gagne.
     p. cm. — (Randy's corner)
 Includes bibliographical references and index.
 ISBN 978-1-58415-986-5 (library bound)
 1. White, Shaun, 1986– – Juvenile literature. 2. Snowboarders — United States — Biography — Juvenile literature. I. Title.
 GV857.S57G34 2011
 796.939092 — dc22
 [B]
                                                                                    2011000730
eBook ISBN: 9781612281544

ABOUT THE AUTHOR: Tammy Gagne has written dozens of books for children, including *What It's Like to Be Pelé* and *Day by Day with LeBron James*. Shaun White is one of her favorite athletes, because he constantly challenges himself with new goals. When he won the gold medal in 2010, Tammy was glued to her television set along with 30 million other people.

PUBLISHER'S NOTE: The following story has been thoroughly researched and to the best of our knowledge represents a true story. While every possible effort has been made to ensure accuracy, the publisher will not assume liability for damages caused by inaccuracies in the data and makes no warranty on the accuracy of the information contained herein. This story has not been authorized or endorsed by Shaun White.

DAY BY DAY WITH

SHAUN
WHITE

Shaun White won the gold medal for the United States in the men's Snowboard Halfpipe at the 2010 Winter Olympics in Vancouver, Canada. He is known all over the world as the Flying Tomato, but he is tired of the nickname. "Someone said I looked like Animal on the drum set from *The Muppet Show*," he said. "Call me Shaun 'Animal' White."

Shaun was born on September 3, 1986, in San Diego, California. When he isn't snowboarding, he can be found on another type of board: a skateboard. He began skateboarding at the age of six and turned professional at age thirteen.

Shaun makes mind-blowing moves look simple, but his early life was not easy. As a baby he had a serious heart condition. He had two operations to correct it. As a young boy, he was bowlegged. He had to wear leg braces every night while he slept. He recovered very well from both of these challenges.

Now Shaun is fearless. He invented many of the snowboarding tricks viewers saw in the 2010 Olympics. He likes to give his moves fun names, like the Cab Double Cork 10, the Double Back Rodeo, and the Switch Back 900.

Shaun spends his days practicing the basics so he can do well in competitions. He likes to eat a nice juicy steak the night before he competes.

GOGGLES

HELMET

CHEST PROTECTOR

Shaun admits that performing snowboarding tricks can be risky. "It's pretty dangerous," he says. "I never attempt something I don't feel confident in. That's a good way to get hurt."

KNEE PADS

WRIST GUARDS

IMPACT SHORTS

When he practiced for the 2010 Olympics,
foam pads were placed at the bottom of his
halfpipe. They protected him whenever he fell.

To get to this super halfpipe, Shaun was airlifted by helicopter and then shuttled by snowmobile. There, he practiced spinning combinations like his Double McTwist 1260.

The pit was made from 8,000 pounds of steel and filled with 7,000 foam blocks.

Shaun's mom and sister come to his competitions to cheer him on. They were there with his father, Roger, and brother, Jesse, when he won gold at his first Olympics in Turin in 2006.

SISTER KARI

DOUBLE MCTWIST 1260

HE IS CLOSE WITH HIS COACH, BUD KEANE.

Shaun won the gold medal in Vancouver after his first run down the halfpipe. He capped off his second run with his Double McTwist 1260, which includes two flips and three and a half spins. He stuck the landing perfectly. Shaun called this second run "a righteous victory lap."

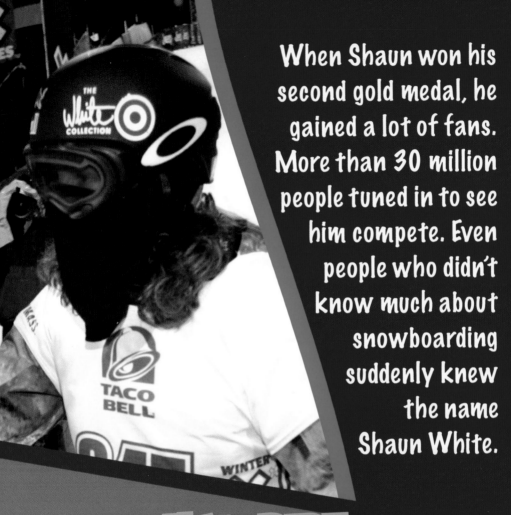

When Shaun won his second gold medal, he gained a lot of fans. More than 30 million people tuned in to see him compete. Even people who didn't know much about snowboarding suddenly knew the name Shaun White.

HALFPIPE

Lip

Deck

Vertical

Transitions

Rider's Right Wall

Rider's Left Wall

Flat

Shaun spends most of his time snowboarding, but there is a lot more to him than sports. He is also a huge music lover. In his spare time, he plays guitar. "I think guitar is the best thing in the world," he says.

Shaun likes to play with other musicians more than by himself.

BROTHER
JESSE

24

SHAUN WHITE

Shaun makes ads for all sorts of big companies—including American Express, Hewlett-Packard, and Red Bull. He also has a clothing line at Target and his own snowboarding videogames.

One of Shaun's role models is skateboarding legend Tony Hawk. The two athletes are also friends. One thing they do together is charity work. Shaun helps Tony raise money to build skate parks around the country.

Shaun also helps St. Jude Children's Hospital. He played foosball with a child named Cameron in the Shaun White Great Room at Target House in Memphis, Tennessee. St. Jude's patients and their families can stay at Target House when kids need long-term treatments.

LOUIE VITO

Shaun loves his teammates. He jokes with them between practices. Besides Shaun, the 2010 U.S. Snowboard Team members were Greg Bretz, Louie Vito, Scott Lago, Hannah Teter, Gretchen Bleiler, Kelly Clark, and Elena Hight.

Would Shaun compete in the Olympics in 2014?

"I've reached my goal with snowboarding," he said. "If skating got into the Olympics, I would be tempted to hold off on shredding for a year and just skate, to make that my new goal."

Either way, we haven't seen the last of Shaun White.

FURTHER READING

Books

Gitlin, Marty. *Shaun White: Snow and Skateboard Champion.* Berkeley Heights, NJ: Enslow Publishers, 2009.

Kennedy, Mike. *Shaun White.* New York: Gareth Stevens Publishing, 2009.

Tieck, Sarah. *Shaun White: Olympic Champion.* Pinehurst, NC: Buddy Books, 2010.

Works Consulted

Dodd, Johnny, and Lorenzo Benet. "Shaun White, Chairman of the Board." *People,* March 15, 2010, Vol. 73, Issue 10.

Gregory, Sean. "Shaun White." *Time,* February 15, 2010, Vol. 175, Issue 6.

Grigoriadis, Vanessa. "Up in the Air." *Rolling Stone,* March 18, 2010, Issue 1100, pp. 40–45.

Kirby, Jason. "On the Wrong Bus with Shaun White." *Maclean's CA,* March 8, 2010, Vol. 123, Issue 8.

Lane, Lori. "Shaun White Wins Olympic Halfpipe Gold Before His Second Run! Shaun White Wins Gold Before Double McTwist 1260." *Associated Content,* February 17, 2010. http://www.associatedcontent.com/article/2712555/shaun_white_wins_olympic_halfpipe_gold.html

Mathai, Raj. "Shaun White Changing His Nickname." *NBC Bay Area,* January 29, 2010.

Tejada, Justin. "Piping Hot." *Sports Illustrated.* January/February 2010, Vol. 22 Issue 1, pp. 18–22.

On the Internet

Kids' Choice Awards 2010
http://www.nick.com/kids-choice-awards/shaun-white-biography.html

Kids' Health—Safety Tips Snowboarding
http://kidshealth.org/parent/firstaid_safe/outdoor/safety_snowboarding.html

Shaun White: Official Site
http://www.shaunwhite.com

INDEX